What's in this book

学习内容 Contents   2

读一读 Read   4

听听说说 Listen and say   12

写一写 Write   16

多元学习 Connections   18

温习 Checkpoint   20

分享 Sharing   22

This book belongs to

T0351528

_____

中国的城市 Cities in China

学习内容 Contents

沟通 Communication

认识中国的主要城市
Learn about the main cities in China

生词 New words

★	想	to want
★	北京	Beijing
★	上海	Shanghai
★	楼	building
★	房子	house
★	地方	place
★	哪儿	where
	城市	city
	长城	Great Wall
	香港	Hong Kong
	像	to be like

背景介绍:
上海、香港和北京是中国
著名的城市,各具特色。

上海

上海

香港

2

北京

句式 Sentence patterns

你想来中国吗？

Do you want to come to China?

你想去哪儿呢？

Where do you want to go?

跨学科学习 Project

不同国家的首都

The capital cities of different countries

文化 Cultures

世界奇观——长城

The Great Wall—one of the Wonders of the World

参考答案：
1 Yes, I have./No, I haven't.
2 I think the cities in China are beautiful/modern.
3 I want to visit Beijing/Shanghai/Hong Kong.

Get ready

1 Have you been to China?

2 What are your impressions of the cities in China?

3 Which city do you want to go in China?

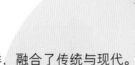

故事大意：
中国的城市风格多样，融合了传统与现代。

上海

北京

chéng shì
城市

xiǎng
想

香港

上海

你想来中国吗？你知道中国有哪些城市吗？

参考问题和答案：
Would you want to visit China? Why? (Yes, because the cities in China are interesting./No, China is too far away.)

北京是中国的首都，是一座历史悠久的文化名城。长城和天安门是北京的名胜古迹。长城是中国古代的军事防御工程。天安门坐落在北京市中心，1949年10月1日，中国的开国大典在天安门举行。此后天安门被设计入国徽，成为了中国的象征之一。

北京是中国的首都。长城和天安门很有名。

参考问题和答案：

1 What are your impressions of Beijing? (Beijing is both modern and traditional. It is beautiful.)

2 What do you think the Great Wall was built for? (It was built for defence against enemies./It was built for sightseeing.)

上海是中国的直辖市，是中国的经济科技中心。上海有大量现代风格的摩天大厦，也有很多老建筑。

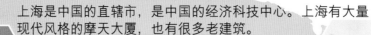

shàng hǎi
上海

陆家嘴金融中心
（左为上海环球金融中心，右为金茂大厦。）

lóu
楼

陆家嘴金融中心
（左侧最高的是东方明珠广播电视塔，右侧最高的是上海中心大厦，现为中国第一，世界第二高楼。）

浦东新区

上海邮政总局

武康大楼

上海浦东发展银行总部

fáng zi
房子

上海有高高的楼，也有很多漂亮的老房子。

参考问题和答案：

1 What are your impressions of Shanghai? (Shanghai is also modern and traditional at the same time, like Beijing.)

2 Which buildings in the picture do you like? (I like the tall and modern buildings./ I like the traditional buildings because they have a western style.)

香港是中国的特别行政区，是一座繁荣的国际化都市。香港有中西文化交融的风景名胜，也有"购物天堂"的美誉。

xiāng gǎng
香港

海洋公园空中缆车

夜晚的维多利亚港湾附近建筑

太平山缆车

天坛大佛

dì fāng
地方

白天的维多利亚港

国际金融中心商场

香港不大，但是有很多好玩的地方。

参考问题和答案：

1 What are your impressions of Hong Kong? (It is an exciting city. I can do many different things there.)
2 Do you like to ride on a cable car or a tram more? (I like the cable car more because it is fun.)

xiàng

像

香港青马大桥

上海南浦大桥

香港维多利亚港

上海外滩

有人觉得香港和上海很像。你觉得呢?

参考问题和答案:

1 Do the highways and the buildings look similar to each other in the pictures? (Yes, they do.)

2 Do you think Hong Kong and Shanghai look similar? (Yes, I do.)

云南大理五华楼

广西阳朔漓江

黑龙江双峰林场（中国雪乡）

nǐ xiǎng qù nǎr ne

你想去哪儿呢？

老北京四合院

北京京剧舞台

香港海滩

中国还有很多有意思的城市。你想去哪儿呢？

参考问题和答案：

Where in China would you like to visit? (I would like to visit Chengdu because I want to see the pandas.)

Let's think

1 Match the tourist attractions to the correct cities.

提醒学生对照第5至8页的内容完成题目。

Beijing

Shanghai

Hong Kong

2 Which city do you want to visit? Draw and talk about it with your friend.

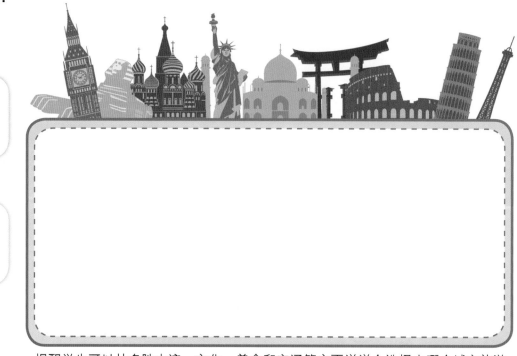

我想去……
因为……

我也喜欢那里，
但是……

提醒学生可以从名胜古迹、文化、美食和交通等方面说说会选择去哪个城市旅游。

New words

02 **1** Learn the new words.

延伸活动：
带领全班学生对三个城市进行投票，每个学生选出最想去的城市，
依照投票结果分三组，各自用新学的词汇描述这个城市。

北京　长城　房子

香港　城市　地方

上海　楼　像

哪儿　想

2 Listen to your teacher and point to
the correct words above.

听听说说 Listen and say

 1 Listen and circle the correct answers.

1 女孩想去哪儿？

    ⓐ 长城

    b 香港

    c 上海

2 男孩想去香港，为什么？

    a 因为那里很好看。

    b 因为香港和上海很像。

    ⓒ 因为香港有很多好玩的地方。

3 男孩在哪儿上课？

    a 红色的楼

    b 红色的房子

    ⓒ 高高的楼

2 Look at the pictures. Listen to the story a

 你和浩浩去上美术课吗？

 是，我们最喜欢美术课。

 我想画长城。长城很高、很长……

第一题录音稿：
1 男孩：明天你想去哪儿？
　女孩：明天我想去长城和天安门。
2 男孩：我想去香港。
　女孩：为什么？
　男孩：因为我可以去山上，去海边，还可以去看熊猫。
3 男孩：前面是我上课的地方。
　女孩：是这个红色的房子吗？
　男孩：不，是那个高高的楼。

你想画什么？

我想画上海的楼和老房子。

你画的长城真像我画的老房子。

二题参考问题和答案：

hy did Ling Ling laugh? (Because she thought the Great Wall
ao Hao drew was similar to the old buildings that she drew.)

3 Tick and say the correct sentences.

北京

- [✓] 她想去北京。
- [ ] 她去想北京。

上海

- [✓] 上海有高高的楼，
  也有很多老房子。
- [ ] 上海有高高的楼，
  有很多老房子也。

提醒学生注意在中文中"也"的位置。
"也"是副词，表达"同样"的意思，
修饰动词时用在动词前。

13

Task

引导学生从美食和建筑风格等角度对比学生的家乡和中国，中国是世界三大美食国之一，拥有八大菜系。中国的建筑艺术历史悠久，城市中保留了传统建筑，也有很多现代摩天大厦。

What is the difference between your hometown and China? Paste your photos and say in Chinese.

我的城市有很多好吃的东西，有……

中国有很多好吃的东西。

Paste your photo here.

中国的楼和房子很……

Paste your photo here.

我的城市的楼和房子很……

Game

Compare the two pictures. Circle the nine differences in the picture on the right.

这个地方不一样。这里的树少了……

引导学生在玩游戏的同时，用所学词汇描述两幅图画的不同，如：这两个房子很像，但是两个窗不一样。

Chant

05 Listen and say.

延伸活动:
学生分四组,以接龙形式每组唱两句,在唱到"中国"、
"北京"、"上海"和"香港"时,大家互相击掌。

中国有很多城市,
你知道这几个吗?
首都北京很古老,
有长城和天安门。
上海真是国际化,
人多车多楼也多。
还有香港这地方,
大家都很喜欢它。

生活用语 Daily expressions

太像了!

So similar!

真没想到。

I never knew that.

写一写 Write

1 Trace and write the characters.

一 十 才 木 札 栌 相 相

相 相 想 想 想

提醒学生，"想"是一个
形声字，"心"是形旁，
"相"是声旁。

一 十 土 圹 圹 地

一 亠 方 方

2 Write and say. 提醒学生，第一个空与思想有关，第二个空与位置有关。

我 <u>想</u> 去上海玩。

我想去这个 <u>地方</u>。

3 Read, circle the wrong words and write the correct ones. There is one mistake in each line.

昨天我们一起丢北京了。　1　___去___

北京有很多好玩的地房，我　2　___方___

最喜欢长城。我们也相去　3　___想___

上海，去看那里高高的楼扣　4　___和___

老房子。

提醒学生一边观察图片一边将段落完整读一遍，理解段落大意后，圈出错误的字
并改正。完成后，再通读改正的段落，看看内容是否正确，文字是否通顺。

拼音输入法 Pinyin input

1 Look at the characters and the typing methods. Say the words.

kuai
1 快　2 哭艾　3 苦艾　⬍

ku'ai
1 酷爱　2 哭艾　3 苦艾　⬍

Some Pinyin syllables have the same letter combination, but they represent one or more characters. We can add the mark (') to break the syllable when the second one starts with 'a', 'e' or 'o'.

2 Add the mark (') to the Pinyin to avoid confusion and write the answers in the boxes. Type the words.

天安门
tiananmen

tian'anmen

西安
xian

xi'an

Cultures 长城是中国古代的军事防御工程，绵延上万里，故又被称作万里长城。长城的修筑历史可追溯至西周时期，遗址跨越15个省市自治区。长城在布局和修筑上充分利用了连绵山峰的地势优势。墙身平均高度7.8米，有些地段高达14米。

1 Do you know one of the Wonders of the World is in China? Learn about the Great Wall.

长城

The Great Wall of China is a series of fortresses built across the historical northern borders of China.

It was used to protect the states from the invasions.

The Great Wall with all of its branches measures about 21,196 km.

2 Imagine you are on the Great Wall. Draw yourself in the picture and answer the questions.

长城怎么样？那儿好玩吗？你累不累？

长城很……

参考表述：
长城很长很大，我喜欢去长城。

北京图中建筑为天安门，它是中国国家象征。伦敦图中主要建筑有大本钟，它是伦敦的标志性建筑。华盛顿图中建筑为美国国会大厦，历届美国总统在此宣誓就职。新德里图中建筑为胡马雍陵，是莫卧儿王朝第二代皇帝胡马雍的陵墓。开罗图中的建筑为金字塔，是古埃及法老的陵墓，是世界八大建筑奇迹之一。堪培拉图中建筑为澳洲国会大厦，它是堪培拉的标志性建筑。

1 Match the capital cities to the countries. Say the names of the cities in Chinese after your teacher.

华盛顿　　　　　　堪培拉　　　　开罗
a Washington, D.C.　　b Canberra　　c Cairo
d New Delhi　　　　　e London　　　f Beijing
新德里　　　　　　　伦敦　　　　　北京

中国　f

英国　e

美国　a

India　d

Egypt　c

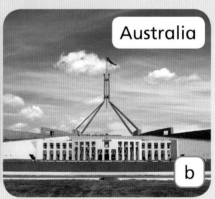
Australia　b

2 Plan a visit to one of the above cities. Fill in the blanks and talk about the city with your friend.

✈ Boarding Pass

👤 名字：＿＿＿＿＿＿

✈ 北京—＿＿＿＿＿＿

📅 ＿＿月＿＿日

✔ ＿＿门　＿＿号

……月……日，我想去……因为那个城市很好玩。那儿的楼和房子也很好看，有新的和旧的……

温习 Checkpoint

学生可以进行分组比赛游戏，由一人提问，另外一人或几人回答。提醒学生先对应图片与问题，回答所有问题后，统计自己答对的题目所对应的分数，计算总分。

1 Answer the questions in Chinese and fill in the sentences. Count the points you can get.

中国的城市

北京	+2	a 这是哪个城市？	+4 e 这个地方在哪个国家？	中
不像	+2	b 新房子和旧房子像吗？	+4 f 他们几点去上海？	四点四十五
上海	+3	c 这些楼在哪个城市？	+5 g 这两个 地 方 在哪儿？	
香港	+3	d 这是香港还是上海？	+5 h 他们 想 去哪儿？	My points:

评核方法：
学生两人一组，互相考察评价表内单词和句子的听说读写。交际沟通部分由老师朗读要求，
学生再互相对话。如果达到了某项技能要求，则用色笔将星星或小辣椒涂色。

2 Work with your friend. Colour the stars and the chillies.

Words	说	读	写
想	☆	☆	☆
北京	☆	☆	🌶
上海	☆	☆	🌶
楼	☆	☆	🌶
房子	☆	☆	🌶
地方	☆	☆	☆
哪儿	☆	☆	🌶
城市	☆	🌶	🌶

Words and sentences	说	读	写
长城	☆	🌶	🌶
香港	☆	🌶	🌶
像	☆	🌶	🌶
你想来中国吗？	☆	☆	🌶
你想去哪儿呢？	☆	☆	🌶

Learn about the main cities in China	☆

3 What does your teacher say?

评核建议：
根据学生课堂表现，分别给予"太棒了！
(Excellent!)"、"不错！(Good!)"或"继续努力！
(Work harder!)"的评价，再让学生圈出左侧对
应的表情，以记录自己的学习情况。

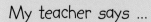
My teacher says ...

分享 Sharing

延伸活动：
1　学生用手遮盖英文，读中文单词，并思考单词意思；
2　学生用手遮盖中文单词，看着英文说出对应的中文单词；
3　学生两人一组，尽量运用中文单词复述第4至9页内容。

Words I remember

想	xiǎng	to want
北京	běi jīng	Beijing
上海	shàng hǎi	Shanghai
楼	lóu	building
房子	fáng zi	house
地方	dì fāng	place
哪儿	nǎr	where
城市	chéng shì	city
长城	cháng chéng	Great Wall
香港	xiāng gǎng	Hong Kong
像	xiàng	to be like

Other words

哪些	nǎ xiē	which
首都	shǒu dū	capital
天安门	tiān ān mén	Tian'anmen
有名	yǒu míng	famous
漂亮	piào liang	beautiful
好玩	hǎo wán	fun
有人	yǒu rén	someone
觉得	jué de	to think
有意思	yǒu yì si	interesting
东西	dōng xi	thing
酷爱	kù ài	to love
西安	xī ān	Xi'an

OXFORD
UNIVERSITY PRESS

Oxford University Press is a department of the University of Oxford.
It furthers the University's objective of excellence in research, scholarship,
and education by publishing worldwide. Oxford is a registered trade mark of
Oxford University Press in the UK and in certain other countries

Published in Hong Kong by
Oxford University Press (China) Limited
39th Floor, One Kowloon, 1 Wang Yuen Street, Kowloon Bay,
Hong Kong

Illustrated by Anne Lee and Wildman

Photographs for reproduction permitted by Dreamstime.com

China National Publications Import & Export (Group) Corporation is an authorized distributor of
Oxford Elementary Chinese.

Please contact content@cnpiec.com.cn or 86-10-65856782

ISBN: 978-0-19-082255-2

10 9 8 7 6 5 4 3 2

Teacher's Edition
ISBN: 978-0-19-082267-5

10 9 8 7 6 5 4 3 2